# JULIUS CAESAR
## GREAT DICTATOR
## OF ROME

Romans hid spikes in pits to trap advancing enemies.

The great Gallic leader Vercingetorix surrendered to Caesar after the siege of Alesia.

Warriors in Britain rode into battle on horse-drawn chariots

A meeting of the Senate, Rome's governing body

Cato, a Roman politician, was thrown out of a Senate meeting for causing trouble.

Egyptian ships on fire in the Great Harbor of Alexandria, Egypt

Caesar died at the foot of a statue of his old enemy, Pompey.

# JULIUS CAESAR

## GREAT DICTATOR
## OF ROME

Written by
RICHARD PLATT

Illustrated by
JOHN JAMES AND JIM ROBINS

A Dorling Kindersley Book

Dorling Kindersley

LONDON, NEW YORK, SYDNEY, DELHI, PARIS,
MUNICH, and JOHANNESBURG

Project Editor  Sadie Smith
Art Editor  Janet Allis
Senior Editor  Scarlett O'Hara
Deputy Managing Art Editor  Vicky Wharton
Managing Editor  Sue Grabham
Senior Managing Art Editor  Julia Harris
Senior DTP Designer  Andrew O'Brien
Picture Researcher  Pernilla Pearce
Jacket Designer  Dean Price
Production  Shivani Pandey
Consultant  Dr. Simon Esmonde Cleary
US Editor  Chuck Wills

First American Edition, 2001
00 01 02 03 04 05 10 9 8 7 6 5 4 3 2 1

Published in the United States by Dorling Kindersley Publishing, Inc.,
95 Madison Avenue, New York, New York 10016

DK Publishing offers special discounts for bulk purchases for sales promotions or
premiums. Specific, large-quantity needs can be met with special editions, including
personalized covers, excerpts of existing guides, and corporate imprints. For more
information, contact Special Markets Department, Dorling Kindersley Publishing, Inc.,
95 Madison Avenue, New York, NY 10016 Fax 800-600-9098

Library of Congress Cataloging-in-Publication Data

Platt, Richard.
    Julius Caesar : Great Dictator of Rome / by Richard Platt.
    p. cm.-- (Dorling Kindersley discoveries)
    Summary: A historical account of Julius Caesar, covering his
personal life, political career, assassination, and the Rome of his
time.
    ISBN 0-7894-6504-3
    1. Caesar, Julius--Juvenile literature 2. Heads of
state--Rome--Biography--Juvenile literature. 3.
Generals--Rome--Biography--Juvenile literature. 4.
Rome--History--Republic, 265–30 B.C.--Juvenile literature. [1. Caesar,
Julius. 2. Heads of state. 3. Generals. 4. Rome--History--Republic,
265–30 B.C.] I. Series.

DG261 .P53 2000
937'.05'092--dc21
                                            00-023668

Reproduced by Colourscan, Singapore
Printed and bound by L.E.G.O., Italy

Additional illustrations by Russell Barnett,
David Ashby, and Sallie Alane Reason

# Contents

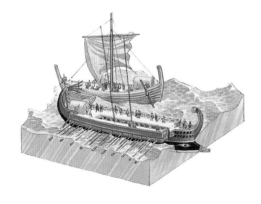

# Caesar's

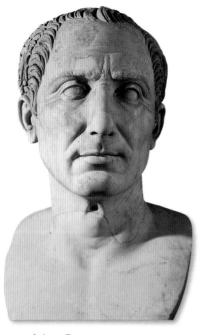

Julius Caesar 100–44 BC

*In the first century BC marble was used to decorate public buildings and temples. Most buildings in Rome were made of brick and stone.*

> "This was the noblest Roman of them all."
>
> From the play *Julius Caesar* by William Shakespeare. Written in 1599

This engraving shows how Rome may have looked when Julius Caesar was born.

# Rome

ROME, 21 CENTURIES AGO, SEEMED TO ITS CITIZENS TO BE THE center of the world. Vast armies kept the city safe from attack and conquered new lands. The citizens ruled themselves as a free republic – they had thrown out their kings 400 years earlier – now the people chose their own rulers. However, all was not well in Rome – in parts of the city discontent simmered. One man became the hero of Romans who wanted a better life. He used their hope and anger to make himself the most powerful leader Rome had known. His name was Julius Caesar.

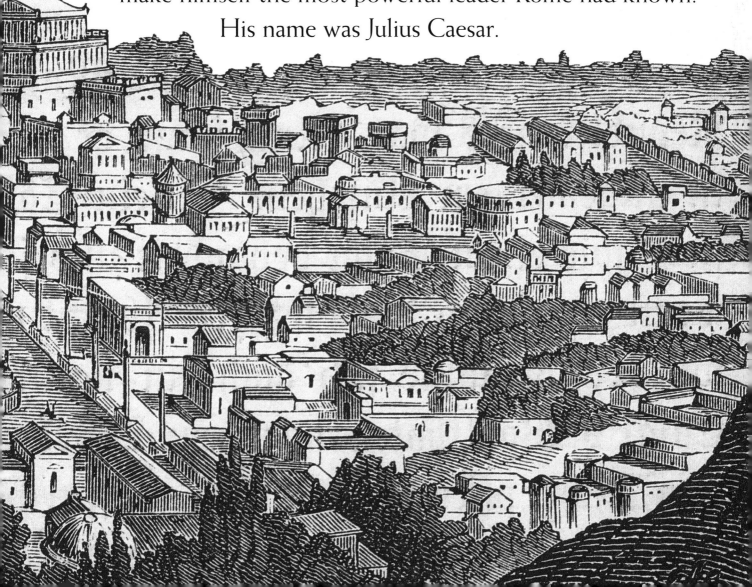

**Building Rome**
Roman engineers and architects created grand temples and other structures in Rome, such as the *Pons Aemilia* bridge (above), completed in 142 BC. This was the first stone bridge across the city's Tiber River. Soaring aqueducts were also built to bring clean drinking water to the city.

**Temples and home shrines**
Religion was an important part of Roman life. Ordinary people worshiped at home. Every house had a small shrine with statues of the home gods. Temple worship was the job of professional priests, though common people might visit to beg a special favor from the gods.

**The army**
The legions – armies of 5–6,000 men – gave Rome military strength and made the Republic rich. Each time these soldiers conquered a new land, loot and tribute (taxes) flowed back to Rome. The importance of the legions gave their commanders great political power.

# THE ROMAN WORLD

IN THE YEAR 100 BC, NO CITY WAS GREATER than Rome. It was the center of the Roman Republic and controlled most of the Mediterranean Sea and surrounding countries. The city was vast, with fine buildings, fashionable shops, and sports arenas. It had modern conveniences such as clean piped water and drainage. However, the city's advantages were not shared equally among its people. A few powerful families, tended by slaves, had most of the wealth. Skilled workers flourished, but Rome was also home to the poor and desperate. They survived on handouts of grain – or by robbing the rich who dodged the traffic in Rome's busy streets.

FEEDING THE POOR
*By regularly handing out free grain to the poor, the rulers of Rome hoped to avoid hunger riots. The quantities were just enough to prevent starvation.*

## STREET LIFE
Busy, impatient people tried to push their way through Rome's crowded streets – just as they do in any modern city. Traffic, street vendors, and entertainers made their progress slow. Stand-up restaurants served snacks, and craftsworkers sold their wares from workshops that opened directly onto the streets.

TRAFFIC JAM
*The crush of carts became so great that when he came to power, Caesar banned them from Rome during the day. Only wagons carrying material to build temples were permitted.*

## RISE OF THE REPUBLIC
In 650 years Rome had grown from a cluster of huts on the banks of the Tiber River into the mightiest power in the world. In Caesar's lifetime it was to become mightier still.

| 1000 BC | 753 BC | 509 BC | 390 BC |
|---|---|---|---|
| Rich farm-land and an easy river crossing made the banks of the Tiber, where Rome now stands, an attractive place to settle. | Roman myth tells how Romulus and Remus founded the city. Abandoned as babies, they were raised by a she-wolf. | Kings ruled Rome at first, but the Roman people threw them out and made Rome a republic (a city ruled by its citizens). | Gauls, from what is now France, attacked Rome and burned down the city. The Romans had to pay in gold to be released. |

France (Gaul)

Spain

Corsica

Italy

Sardinia

*Rome*

Greece

Turkey

Carthage

Sicily

MEDITERRANEAN SEA

Africa

The green shaded areas on this modern map show the areas ruled by the Romans in 100 BC

## ROMANS REDRAW THE MAP

Rome's expansion beyond Italy began when Roman soldiers battled with North African rivals in Carthage in the first Punic War (264–241 BC). In winning this fight, Romans learned the art of war at sea. Roman navies later used their skills to take control of the Mediterranean Sea.

*A wealthy Roman lady browses the shops with her slaves.*

A litter

*A poet entertains a group of passersby.*

SAFE CROSSING
*The streets of Rome were paved with lava slabs and had stepping stones for crossing.*

## SLAVE TRANSPORT

Most townhouse slaves worked as servants – carrying a litter was one of many tasks. Well-educated Greek slaves were more expensive and worked as doctors, tutors, or librarians. They had much better lives than those slaves who worked in chain gangs on Roman farms.

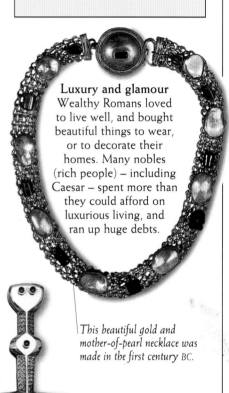

**Luxury and glamour**
Wealthy Romans loved to live well, and bought beautiful things to wear, or to decorate their homes. Many nobles (rich people) – including Caesar – spent more than they could afford on luxurious living, and ran up huge debts.

*This beautiful gold and mother-of-pearl necklace was made in the first century BC.*

**Violent city**
Rome could be a dangerous place. Violent robbery was common on the streets, and after dark no wealthy Roman traveled without bodyguards. Violence was also an accepted part of Roman politics. For example, in 133 BC, opponents of Tiberius Gracchus attacked him in the people's assembly (parliament), killing him and his 300 supporters.

| 338 BC | 264–241 BC | 100 BC |
|---|---|---|
| Rome expanded quickly, becoming Italy's most powerful city. After defeating its neighbors in the Great Latin War, Rome ruled all of Italy. | It took Rome three wars to defeat African rival, Carthage. Enemy general Hannibal crossed the Alps with elephants to attack Rome. | Gaius Julius Caesar was born in a district of Rome. He grew up in an unstable nation that could no longer govern its wealthy but distant provinces. |

**Descended from the gods**
Caesar's clan, the Julii, were *patricians* – members of a privileged circle of Rome's oldest families. According to legend, Caesar was descended from Venus, the Roman goddess of love. More recent ancestors had been consuls. This meant Caesar was a noble, one of Rome's ruling classes.

**School for rulers**
Like other upper-class boys, Caesar learned public speaking and the Greek language. His tutor was from Gaul (now France). Some wealthy Roman families hired a private tutor for their sons. These tutors were called *pedagogi* and were well-educated Greek slaves.

# FACT file

- When Caesar was aged between 9 and 13 years old a civil war divided Italy. Around 300,000 people died fighting for their rights as Roman citizens.

- Scholars cannot agree on Caesar's date of birth, though most accept 100 BC as the most likely date.

- Nothing is known of Caesar's life between 73 and 69 BC.

- Like many would-be politicians, Caesar was in debt from an early age.

# ESCAPE AND CAPTURE

ONE SUMMER'S DAY IN 100 BC, THE CRY of a newborn baby echoed from the Caesar's house. His parents called the baby boy Gaius, but today his clan name, Julius, is better known. Caesar grew up in a world of politics, and by the age of 16 his strong views had made him an enemy of Rome's ruler, Sulla. To avoid trouble he fled Rome, and lived as an outlaw for three years. When he returned in 78 BC, Caesar worked as a lawyer. In court he practiced oratory (speaking skills) which he would later use to charm the Roman people. In 75 BC, Caesar left Rome again. This time on a trip that became a dangerous adventure.

## PIRATE ATTACK
Caesar traveled to Greece, perhaps to escape from enemies he had made as a lawyer in Rome, but certainly to rest and study. Whatever the reason, the trip did not go according to plan. Close to the Greek island of Pharmacusa pirates attacked the ship on which he was traveling.

*The pirates would have rammed Caesar's ship to disable it.*

## A RICH PRIZE
Caesar was just the sort of Roman the pirates were seeking to capture. His fine clothing and good manners showed he was from a wealthy family. The pirates guessed his friends and relatives would ransom him – pay money for his release.

CAPTURED!
*Pirates sold most of the people they captured as slaves, or used them to row their ships. Only the wealthiest captives were held to ransom.*

*Anyone who resisted capture was killed by the pirates.*

## ISLAND PRISONER

Caesar's captors demanded a ransom of 20 talents – roughly 20 soldiers' wages for a year. Sneering that this was not enough for someone of his importance, Caesar told them to ask for 50 talents, and servants were sent to fetch the money. While he waited to be released, he joined in with the pirates' games, and read them poems and speeches he had written.

### COMPANIONS IN CAPTIVITY
*Caesar's doctor and two servants watched as he insulted his captors, calling them "illiterate barbarians." He even told the pirates to keep quiet when he wanted to sleep.*

### "I'LL BE BACK"
Five weeks later the ransom arrived and the pirates released Caesar. Before leaving his captors, Caesar vowed he would return and kill them all. The pirates laughed at this, but it was no joke. Caesar kept his promise and soon returned. He got back his ransom money, rounded up the pirates, and had them crucified (hung from crosses).

### CITY JAIL
*Before being crucified, the pirates were held in a jail in the great city of Pergamum.*

### MERCIFUL DEATH
*Crucifixion was a slow, painful way to die. In a surprising act of mercy, Caesar had the pirates' throats slit before crucifying them.*

"This young man who is so precious to you will one day overthrow the aristocratic party, which you and I have fought hard to defend."

Consul Sulla's words to Caesar's supporters, quoted by Roman historian Suetonius in *The Lives of the Caesars*, written c. AD 110

Carving of a Roman marriage ceremony

### First marriage
When he was 16, Caesar married Cornelia. He hoped the match would help his career – Cornelia's father, Cinna, had led the winning side in the civil war that had recently split Italy. However, soon after the wedding Cinna was murdered. His enemy, Sulla, swept to power and ordered Caesar to divorce Cornelia. Caesar refused and fled Rome.

# The family home

NOTHING REMAINS of Caesar's family home in Rome. However, well-preserved remains of other town houses suggest that it was probably built on two floors surrounding a courtyard called an *atrium*.

### Courtyard and garden
Roman town houses had few windows looking out into the public street. Instead, air and light came in from the private *atrium*. Wealthier families extended the house by adding more rooms around a second courtyard, the *peristylium*, which was planted as a garden.

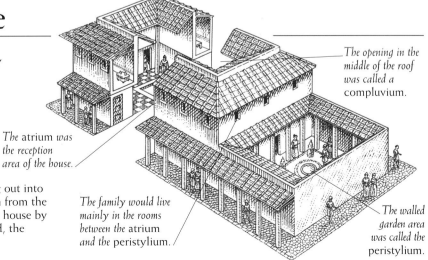

*The atrium was the reception area of the house.*

*The family would live mainly in the rooms between the atrium and the peristylium.*

*The opening in the middle of the roof was called a compluvium.*

*The walled garden area was called the peristylium.*

A coin made to mark
the funeral
of Julia

## Funeral speech

When his aunt Julia died in 68 BC, Caesar spoke at her funeral. Julia was the widow of Marius, leader of the *Populares* political group (the people's party). Caesar gained the support of the *Populares* by praising their dead leader and by displaying his picture at the funeral. Caesar also used the speech to draw attention to himself and his good family background.

# POLITICAL AMBITION

CAESAR GREATLY ADMIRED THE GREEK leader Alexander the Great (356–323 BC). By the time Alexander was Caesar's age (30) he had built a huge empire and become the most powerful man in the world. What had Caesar achieved? He was a member of the College of Pontiffs, which organized worship in Rome, and he was a tribune – a minor military officer. By 68 BC, Caesar was a quaestor (an administrator) far away in Spain. However, these positions meant nothing to Caesar – he was an ambitious man who longed for greater power. After spending only a few weeks in Spain, Caesar returned to Rome, where he was determined to make his mark.

CHEAP SEATS
*Ordinary spectators watched from wooden stands set up around the Roman Forum.*

GOOD PROTECTION
*The Samnite gladiator wore lots of armor, including a sturdy helmet.*

The Rostra

## FORUM GAMES

In Republican Rome, gladiatorial combats usually took place in the Roman Forum. Of all entertainments, free gladiator shows were the most popular with the people. In 66 BC Caesar was elected as a *curule aedile*. This position made Caesar responsible for Rome's streets, traffic, water supplies, and markets. However, the most exciting responsibility this position offered was the organization of the forum games.

BLADE FIGHTER
*The Thracian was a lightly-armed gladiator. He used a curved dagger in combat.*

## FIGHT FOR SUPPORT

65 BC

In a show given in honor of his father in 65 BC, Caesar hired 320 gladiators. He borrowed huge sums of money in order to throw the most lavish games ever seen in Rome – the gladiators all wore silver armor. This fabulous free show would guarantee the support of the people in future elections.

THE BEST SEATS
*Caesar and other important politicians would sit in comfort on the Rostra. A silk awning protected them from the sun.*

THE NET MAN
*The retiarius used a net to trip his opponent. His other weapon was a three-forked trident.*

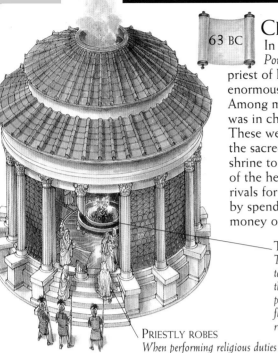

## CHIEF PRIEST

**63 BC** In 63 BC Caesar was voted *Pontifex Maximus*, the chief priest of Rome. This job gave him enormous power and influence. Among many other duties, Caesar was in charge of the Vestal Virgins. These were young girls who tended the sacred fire at the important shrine to Vesta, the Roman goddess of the hearth. Caesar beat his two rivals for the job of *Pontifex Maximus* by spending huge amounts of money on bribing the voters.

THE TEMPLE OF VESTA
*The sacred fire burned in this circular temple. Any Vestal Virgin who allowed the flame to die out would be severely punished. By burning constantly, the flames represented the idea that Roman rule would last forever.*

PRIESTLY ROBES
*When performing religious duties Caesar had to wear a hooded robe. This was the traditional outfit for a priest.*

> "he [Caesar] showed himself perfectly ready to serve and flatter everybody, even ordinary people, and shrank from no speech or action in order to get possession of the objects for which he strove."
>
> Roman historian, Dio Cassius in *Roman History*, written in the 3rd century AD

STOP THE COACH!
*Caesar's creditors did not want him to leave Rome, because they believed he would not pay his debts if he was far away in Spain.*

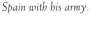

ARMY CONVOY
*Caesar traveled into Spain with his army.*

# FACT file

- In 62 BC Caesar was in such a hurry to escape his creditors that he left Rome before the Senate had formally awarded him the province of Farther Spain.
- The cost of sponsoring a gladiator show was at least 720,000 sesterces – enough to buy 30 large country houses.
- When he left Rome, Caesar had debts of 55 million sesterces – the wages of Rome's entire army for two months.

## ESCAPING DEBT

**62 BC** Caesar's luck continued in 62 BC when he was elected praetor for a year. This was Rome's best government job, apart from consul. After a year in office, a praetor was made the governor of a province. Caesar was awarded Farther Spain, but he nearly did not get there. He had huge debts and the people to whom he owed money stopped his carriage when he tried to leave Rome. They released him only when his rich friend, Crassus, promised to pay them if Caesar could not.

**Political enemies**
Writer and orator Cicero (104–43 BC) was consul in 63 BC when Caesar's political career was just beginning. Caesar found Cicero a powerful opponent in Senate meetings and tried several times to form an alliance with him. Cicero mistrusted Caesar and refused. Forced out of politics, Cicero attacked Caesar in his writings.

# On the Road

"All things were now possible to Caesar by reason of his large army, his great riches, and his readiness to serve everyone."

Roman historian Appian, in his book *Civil Wars*, written C. AD 2

*When he surrendered, the Gallic leader Vercingetorix expected to be executed instantly. However, Caesar spared his life — for the moment.*

Vercingetorix throws down his arms at the feet of Julius Caesar, a painting by Lionel Noel Royer, 1899

# to Power

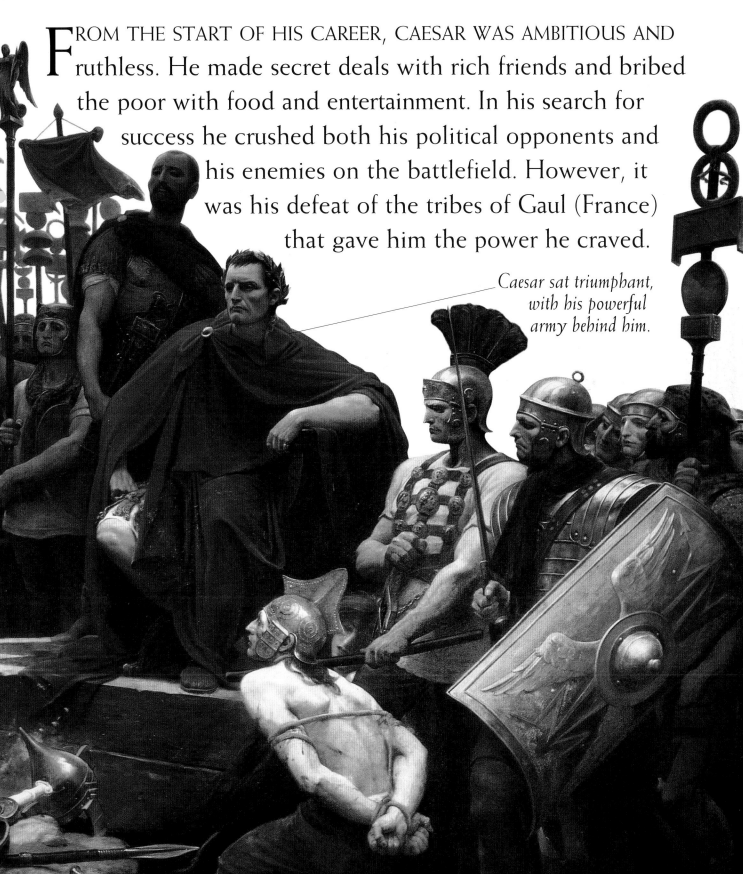

FROM THE START OF HIS CAREER, CAESAR WAS AMBITIOUS AND ruthless. He made secret deals with rich friends and bribed the poor with food and entertainment. In his search for success he crushed both his political opponents and his enemies on the battlefield. However, it was his defeat of the tribes of Gaul (France) that gave him the power he craved.

*Caesar sat triumphant, with his powerful army behind him.*

The *Senate* was chosen from Rome's best families.

*Praetors* were in charge of justice.

*Aediles* were responsible for the upkeep of the city.

*Tribunes* were elected by the people.

Two *consuls* were elected for a year at a time.

### Who ruled Rome?

Power in Rome was divided between the voting Assembly of the people and the Senate, which included consuls and other officials. Anyone with powerful friends or a relative who was a consul had a better chance of gaining a position of power.

# LEADER OF THE REPUBLIC

AT LAST, IN 59 BC, CAESAR BECAME consul. Years of groveling, bribing, and making deals had paid off. He was now one of Rome's two most important politicians. Unfortunately, the other was his rival, Bibulus. Consuls had to approve each other's plans, so Bibulus could stop Caesar from using his power. With the backing of important men, Caesar schemed to outwit Bibulus. He decided to use his oratory (speaking skills) to win over the Senate, Rome's aristocrats. If this failed, Caesar plotted to use his popularity with the common people to get his own way.

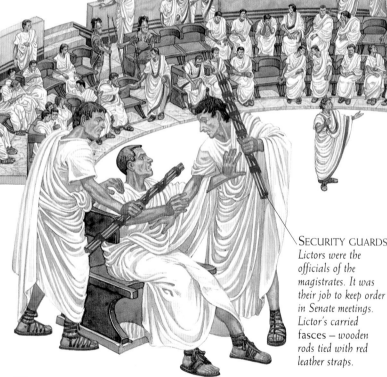

ROBES OF POWER
*In Senate meetings officials would wear the* toga praetexta *– a toga decorated with a broad purple stripe. This could only be worn by citizens of Rome.*

SECURITY GUARDS
*Lictors were the officials of the magistrates. It was their job to keep order in Senate meetings. Lictor's carried* fasces – *wooden rods tied with red leather straps.*

## CAESAR'S LAND LAW

On his first day as consul, Caesar read his land law to the Senate. It was very cleverly written and seemed to be fair to both rich and poor. Senators knew they would earn the hatred of the Roman people if they opposed the law. No one opposed it, but no one supported it either.

## THE OPPOSITION

Only one senator, Marcus Cato, tried to stop the law. He did this by talking nonstop so that the debate would run out of time. Cato constantly opposed Caesar because he saw that Caesar's increasing power threatened the strength of the Republic. Frustrated by the delay, Caesar ordered officials to drag Cato off to jail.

**MARCUS CRASSUS**
*In the past, the immensely wealthy Marcus Crassus (c. 115–53 BC) had loaned Caesar money. In exchange, Caesar promised to help Crassus with his supporters' tax debts in Asia.*

"*...he [Caesar] is a master of eloquence...in respect to voice, gesture, and the speaker's whole physique, [he] possesses a certain noble quality.*"

Roman historian Dio Cassius, in *Roman History*, written in the 3rd century AD

Calpurnia

Pompeia

**New wife, old wife**
Roman politicians chose wives who could improve their career opportunities. Caesar married his second wife, Pompeia, for her fortune. But when a man disguised as a woman sneaked into their house, rumors circulated that Pompeia was being unfaithful to Caesar. Though he did not believe the rumors, Caesar used the scandal as an excuse to divorce her and marry Calpurnia, the daughter of a future consul.

## THE ALLIES
During the debate, Caesar asked two important politicians, Pompey and Crassus, to speak in favor of the law. Their support shocked everyone, because until then the three men had been rivals for power. Nicknamed the *triumvirate*, (gang of three) the allies began to control Rome.

## SUCCESS AT LAST!
When the Senate would not approve his law, Caesar appealed directly to the people's Assembly. Caesar used violence to silence any opposition – when Bibulus tried to oppose the law, he was beaten up by the crowd, which included many of Pompey's soldiers. Caesar's tactics worked, and his law was passed.

**GENERAL POMPEY**
*Pompey the Great (106–28 BC) was one of the most brilliant generals of his time. He was also a vital ally for Caesar. Pompey seemed certain to stay loyal to Caesar when he married Caesar's daughter.*

*In the confusion, a basket of dung was poured over Bibulus!*

**MEETING PLACE**
*Roman senators met to make laws in the curia (Senate house). This building was in the center of Rome.*

*Bibulus tried to stop Caesar's law by saying he feared bad omens in the skies – a traditional way to stop a meeting.*

**MASS GATHERING**
*The meetings of the people's Assembly were so large that they had to take place outside, close to the forum (marketplace).*

**The Gallic campaign**
Caesar's command of the Roman territory of Cisalpine Gaul gave him the chance to conquer neighboring lands. On the weak excuse of controlling migrating German people, Caesar marched into Gaul. He extended this campaign as far north as Britain.

## Bridges

IN THE FOURTH YEAR of his Gallic campaign, Caesar put on a show of strength to impress his enemies. He ordered his soldiers to build the world's biggest bridge, across the wide Rhine River. It took his mighty army only ten days to build.

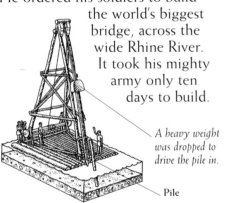

*A heavy weight was dropped to drive the pile in.*

Pile

**1** To support the bridge, Caesar's men drove piles (heavy wooden stakes) into the stony river bed, perhaps using a floating pile driver.

*The bridge platform was as wide as a tennis court.*

**2** Engineers linked the piles with crosspieces and built a platform across. Further stakes upstream stopped floating logs from destroying the bridge.

# RAID AND CONQUER

CAESAR WAS FURIOUS. "MY ONLY subjects will be swine and oxen!" he complained. To spite Caesar, the senators had made him ruler of worthless fields and woodland. Insulted by being given such an unimportant area to govern, Caesar used his popularity with the people once more. He appealed to their Assembly and was given the provinces of Illyricum (the east coast of the Adriatic Sea) and Cisalpine Gaul as well. Then the governor of Transalpine Gaul died, and Caesar grabbed that, too. In spring 58 BC, he left for Gaul, determined to win new lands and wealth for Rome, and of course, a little glory for himself.

*Oars enabled light Roman galleys to move fast.*

A Veneti ship

A Roman galley

RIGGING ATTACK
*Armed with hooks on long poles, Romans snapped the ropes that held up the leather sails.*

### SEA BATTLE
56 BC
When the Veneti people of northwest Gaul rebelled against the Roman advance, Caesar attacked them at sea. The battle took place at Quiberon Bay. The Gallic ships were too strong to be rammed (the usual Roman naval tactic), so instead Caesar's men cut down their sails.

### LONG CAMPAIGN
When he left Rome in 58 BC, Caesar had no idea how long it would take to conquer Gaul. Resistance to Roman rule lasted eight years.

| 58 BC | 57 BC |
|---|---|
| Caesar became governor of Illyricum, Cisalpine Gaul, and Transalpine Gaul. The Roman army massacred 258,000 Helvetii people. | Caesar subdued the Belgic people in northern Gaul. Crassus, his ally, conquered Normandy and Brittany. |

> "...there isn't a grain of silver on the island nor any prospect of loot apart from captives, and I fancy you won't expect any of them to be highly qualified in literature and music!"
>
> From Cicero's letter describing the British to his friend Atticus, c. July 1, 54 BC

## Horned helmet
This British helmet was found in London's Thames River – evidence that the British wore armor in battle. However, a horned helmet like this one was more likely to have been worn for ceremonial occasions.

*This helmet was made from a mixture of copper and tin.*

*British fighters hid in the woods before launching their attack.*

*Warriors in Britain painted their skin blue to give themselves a wild appearance in battle.*

## TREASURE ISLAND?

**54 BC** Rumors of pearls, gold, and silver tempted Caesar to the shores of Britain in 55 and 54 BC. The first expedition was not very successful, but Caesar returned in 54 BC with a larger army. As his troops were setting up camp, the British stormed out of the woods and launched a surprise attack. The Romans had been caught off guard. Despite this, they still managed to win the battle.

*The Roman camp*

*This Celtic torc was worn around the neck.*

*Roman soldiers had not finished digging the ditch and bank that usually protected their camps.*

*British charioteers drove the warriors into the battle.*

### Master crafts
Artists in Britain crafted beautiful jewelry, like this torc, out of electrum – a mixture of silver and gold. Cicero and other Romans thought the British were unskilled savages, but they were clearly mistaken.

## CHARIOT ATTACK
The British warriors broke through Roman defenses using their fast-moving chariots. Agile warriors would sometimes leap off the chariot in order to fight on foot. This style of attack caused havoc and confusion in the Roman camp.

| 56 BC | 55 BC | 54 BC | 53 BC | 52 BC |
|---|---|---|---|---|
| The Veneti people in north-west Gaul revolted. Caesar suppressed them in a naval battle in Quiberon Bay. | Caesar's army slaughtered thousands of immigrant Germans, bridged the Rhine, and made its first raid on Britain. | Gauls attacked the Roman garrison at Tongeren in northeast Gaul and killed Roman troops. A second raid on Britain was made. | Caesar's army put down numerous revolts in Gaul. Acco, the leader of one of them, was flogged to death in front of other Gallic leaders. | Caesar and his army finally conquered Gaul with a victorious siege at Alesia. |

# REVOLT AND REPRESSION

WAS CAESAR IN TROUBLE? IN 52 BC THE GAULS were fighting against their Roman rulers – and they seemed to be winning. It was a humiliating change of fortune for Caesar. He had written in 57 BC that his operations had "…brought peace throughout Gaul." How wrong he was – five years of rebellion followed. Now, almost all of Gaul had joined the powerful Arverni people to fight the Romans. The Arverni leader, Vercingetorix, led the Gauls in several brilliant victories. But then he made a terrible mistake. He mounted an attack on the marching Roman army. The Romans fought back ferociously, and the Arverni were forced to retreat to their fortress stronghold of Alesia.

*A coin made by the Arverni people shows their leader, Vercingetorix.*

**Heroic leader**
Vercingetorix led Gallic people in a rebellion that almost ended Roman rule of Gaul. In his book *The Gallic Wars*, Caesar expressed a respect for the great leader, describing him as "a man of boundless energy."

Outer line of Roman fortifications

Roman fortifications

Oserain River

## THE ROMAN SIEGE
The Romans surrounded the fort of Alesia and began preparations for a siege. Caesar's army was now on the attack, but soon it faced a double threat – Vercingetorix's army inside Alesia, and relief forces coming to Vercingetorix's aid from outside the fort.

*More than 900 of these towers were built to guard the outer wall.*

*Walls were topped with wickerwork battlements.*

*Circular pits hid sharp stakes.*

*Brushwood concealed vicious upward-pointing spikes.*

## DITCHES AND TRAPS
When the Roman defenses were complete, they encircled Alesia. An inner ring of ditches, fences, and deadly traps stopped Gauls from getting out to obtain food. The outer ring of defenses was built at speed when Caesar learned of the advance of the Gallic reinforcements towards the town.

*By diverting the rivers, Caesar filled large ditches with water.*

*Deep ditches slowed down attackers. This gave the Roman soldiers time to rush to where the Gauls were attempting to break through the defenses.*

# Roman missiles

WHEN ROMAN TROOPS fought from fortifications they used heavy machines to hurl arrows and rocks at the enemy.

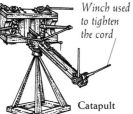

*Sling holding the object to be hurled*

*Onager*

### Small catapult
Caesar's troops drove back the Gallic warriors by firing heavy rocks from a catapult much like this one. It had a winch that pulled back the cord holding the missile.

*Winch used to tighten the cord*

### The *onager*
Springs of braided animal gristle powered this heavier catapult. It was nicknamed the *onager* (donkey) because it kicked violently each time it fired a missile.

*Catapult*

> "So soon did so vast an army dissolve and vanish like a ghost or dream, the greatest part of them being killed upon the spot."
>
> Roman historian Plutarch describing the defeat of the Gallic army at the siege of Alesia, in his book *The Parallel Lives*, written c. AD 75

## THE BIG BATTLE
With 250,000 Gallic troops surrounding the outer ring of the Roman fortifications, Vercingetorix launched his attack, beating back the 70,000 Romans. On the fourth day of battle Caesar led a counterattack, causing the reinforcement forces to flee.

HILL-TOP TOWN
*The town of Alesia stood at the top of a hill between two rivers.*

HELP ARRIVES
*Vercingetorix's reinforcements arrived and attacked the outer ring of Roman fortifications.*

*A Gaul falling on a Roman spike, called a "spur."*

*Ose River*

Inner line of Roman fortifications

*Gallic soldiers rushed out from inside Alesia to attack the inner ring of Roman fortifications.*

*Along the weakest side of their defenses the Gauls had added a wall with a ditch below it.*

DEFEATED LEADER
*In a gesture of surrender, Vercingetorix laid down his weapons at the feet of Caesar.*

Gallic defenses

## DEFENDING THE FORT
Inside Alesia the Gauls prepared to defend themselves. Vercingetorix had sent 10,000 horsemen to get help. Desperately short of food, the defenders considered killing and eating anyone in the town who could not fight. Eventually the soldiers decided to throw the elderly and infirm out of the fort to fend for themselves.

SOLDIER'S REWARD
*To thank his troops for their bravery, Caesar gave each of his soldiers a Gallic warrior as a slave.*

## VICTORY FOR THE ROMANS
Vercingetorix realized he was beaten. Caesar's army had succeeded in defeating two Gallic armies – those inside the fort, and those who attacked the Roman defenses from the outside. Vercingetorix called together the Gallic chiefs and suggested that they could make peace, by handing him – or his body – over to the Romans. The Gauls surrendered and Vercingetorix became Caesar's prisoner.

> "Even yet we may draw back; but cross yon little bridge, and the whole issue is with the sword."
>
> Julius Caesar, quoted by Roman historian Suetonius in *The Lives of the Caesars*, written C. AD 110

In 49 BC, Caesar commanded a loyal and well-trained army – just what he needed for the battles to come.

# Crossing the Rubicon

CAESAR'S VICTORIES IN
Gaul made him rich
and powerful. Now he
was ready to take on his enemies in Rome.
Under Roman law, he could not lead his army
into Italy. The River Rubicon marked Gaul's
border with Italy, and when Caesar took his
soldiers across, he knew that there could
only be one result – war.

This engraving of Caesar
is one of a series made
by French artist
S. D. Mirys c. 1800.

# STRUGGLE FOR POWER

"LET THE DICE FLY HIGH!" SHOUTED Caesar as he crossed the Rubicon River. He meant that he was taking a big gamble. Senators in Rome feared Caesar's growing power and ordered him to give up his army. Caesar was not about to do this, but he had lost two powerful allies. Crassus had died in battle, and Pompey was now leading the army in Rome against Caesar's soldiers. Many Romans supported Caesar as he marched toward Rome – they opposed the old way of governing the Republic. The struggle for power between Caesar and Pompey divided Romans in a civil war – a war that set Roman against Roman.

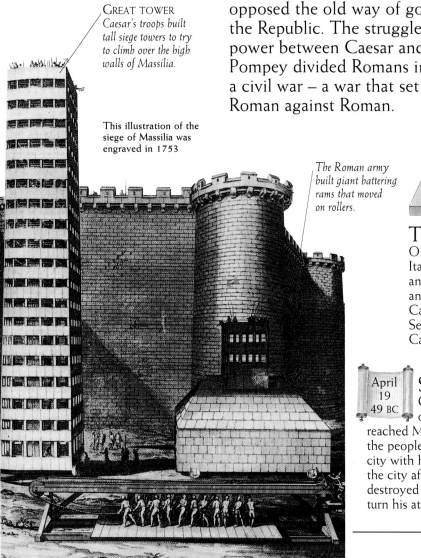

**Pompey – ally turned enemy**
Caesar had always suspected that Pompey's loyalty was weak. He tried to strengthen their alliance by marrying his daughter Julia to Pompey. When Julia died in childbirth, Pompey and Caesar were no longer bound by family ties. Pompey now switched his support to senators who opposed Caesar.

**GREAT TOWER**
*Caesar's troops built tall siege towers to try to climb over the high walls of Massilia.*

This illustration of the siege of Massilia was engraved in 1753

*The Roman army built giant battering rams that moved on rollers.*

GAUL

**MASSILIA, GAUL**
**APRIL 19, 49 BC**
*Caesar captured the city of Massilia.*

**ILERDA, SPAIN**
**AUGUST 27, 49 BC**
*Caesar cornered troops loyal to Pompey at Ilerda.*

AFRICA

**Key to Caesar's route**
1. *Campaign in Italy* 49 BC
2. *Campaign in Spain and Gaul* 49 BC
   out        back
3. *Chasing Pompey* 48 BC

## THE GREAT CHASE
On hearing of Caesar's advance south through Italy, Pompey fled Rome. Caesar first destroyed any opposition in Italy. He then turned to Gaul and Spain to crush Pompey's supporters there. Caesar then pursued Pompey across the Adriatic Sea. Eventually they clashed at Pharsalus, where Caesar was victorious, and Pompey fled to Egypt.

April
19
49 BC
## SIEGE OF MASSILIA
Caesar's campaign to crush support for Pompey outside Italy first took him to Gaul. When he reached Massilia (now Marseilles, in France), Caesar ordered the people to support him. They refused, and defended their city with help from Pompey's officers. Caesar captured the city after a long siege. He then traveled to Spain and destroyed his opponents there. Now Caesar was able to turn his attention to chasing Pompey.

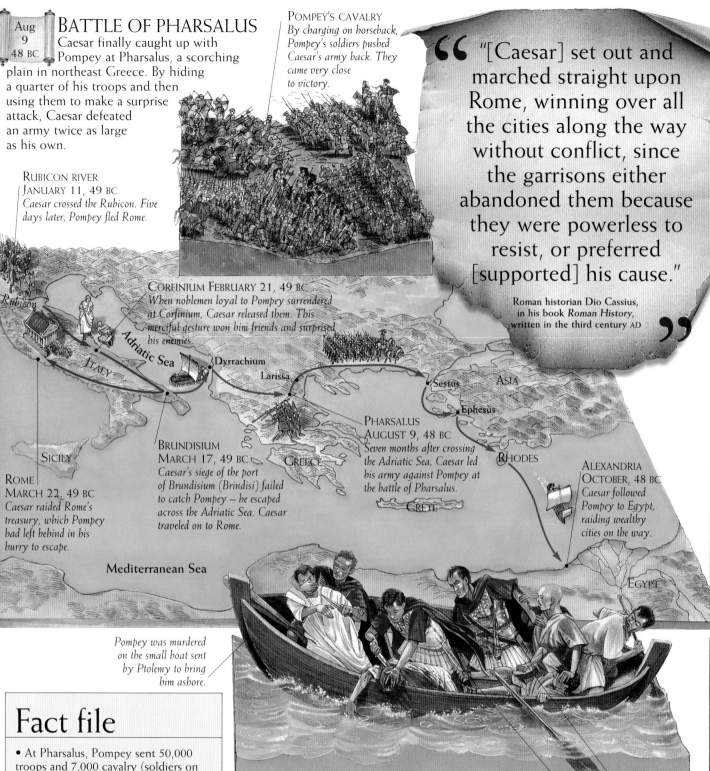

## BATTLE OF PHARSALUS

Aug 9 48 BC

Caesar finally caught up with Pompey at Pharsalus, a scorching plain in northeast Greece. By hiding a quarter of his troops and then using them to make a surprise attack, Caesar defeated an army twice as large as his own.

POMPEY'S CAVALRY
By charging on horseback, Pompey's soldiers pushed Caesar's army back. They came very close to victory.

RUBICON RIVER
JANUARY 11, 49 BC
Caesar crossed the Rubicon. Five days later, Pompey fled Rome.

CORFINIUM FEBRUARY 21, 49 BC
When noblemen loyal to Pompey surrendered at Corfinium, Caesar released them. This merciful gesture won him friends and surprised his enemies.

"[Caesar] set out and marched straight upon Rome, winning over all the cities along the way without conflict, since the garrisons either abandoned them because they were powerless to resist, or preferred [supported] his cause."

Roman historian Dio Cassius, in his book *Roman History*, written in the third century AD

Rubicon

Adriatic Sea

ITALY

Dyrrachium

Larissa

Sestus

ASIA

Ephesus

PHARSALUS
AUGUST 9, 48 BC
Seven months after crossing the Adriatic Sea, Caesar led his army against Pompey at the battle of Pharsalus.

RHODES

SICILY

GREECE

CRETE

ALEXANDRIA
OCTOBER, 48 BC
Caesar followed Pompey to Egypt, raiding wealthy cities on the way.

BRUNDISIUM
MARCH 17, 49 BC
Caesar's siege of the port of Brundisium (Brindisi) failed to catch Pompey – he escaped across the Adriatic Sea. Caesar traveled on to Rome.

ROME
MARCH 22, 49 BC
Caesar raided Rome's treasury, which Pompey had left behind in his hurry to escape.

Mediterranean Sea

EGYPT

Pompey was murdered on the small boat sent by Ptolemy to bring him ashore.

Achillas

BETRAYAL
Pompey was stabbed in the back by one of his former officers, Septimus, who may have been bribed to do the job.

## Fact file

• At Pharsalus, Pompey sent 50,000 troops and 7,000 cavalry (soldiers on horseback) into battle. Caesar's soldiers numbered 23,000, including only 1,000 cavalry. It was the biggest Roman-against-Roman battle ever fought.

• Up to 15,000 of Pompey's troops died on the battlefield at Pharsalus. Caesar may have lost as many as 1,200 soldiers.

• After the battle of Pharsalus, Caesar found Pompey's tent abandoned and ate a meal that had been prepared for his rival.

## DEATH OF POMPEY

Sept 28 48 BC

After his defeat at Pharsalus, Pompey traveled to Alexandria, in Egypt. He believed the Egyptians would take his side against Caesar, and perhaps thought that he could bully their boy-king, Ptolemy, into supporting him. It was a fatal mistake. Achillas, Ptolemy's commander-in-chief, was sent to collect Pompey from his ship as it approached Alexandria. Pompey was expecting a warm welcome – instead, he was brutally murdered.

Caesar would have to unite them to bring back peace. He started by forgiving many who had fought against him. Then he treated the people of Rome to a spectacular triumph. Plundering defeated lands had made Caesar very rich, so he spent lavishly. His ten-day triumph at the end of September 46 BC would be bigger and better than anything Romans had ever seen before.

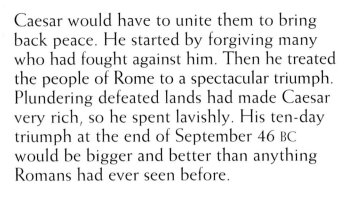

*Cleopatra's 15-month-old son Caesarion was probably Caesar's child.*

Ptolemy 14th

## SPECIAL GUESTS

Caesar's sweetheart Cleopatra watched the Egyptian triumph with her son Caesarion and 11-year-old Ptolemy 14th, brother of Cleopatra and Ptolemy 13th. (Ptolemy 13th had died fighting Caesar.) All three were guests at Caesar's mansion near Rome.

### MODEL LIGHTHOUSE
*A huge model of the Pharos lighthouse of Egypt was paraded through the streets.*

The Egyptian triumph

### EXOTIC CREATURES
*The Egyptian parade featured giraffes, which Roman crowds had never seen before.*

## FACT file

• Caesar claimed that 1,192,000 enemies of Rome had been killed in the four victories. It is likely he was exaggerating.
• The triumph cost 600 million sesterces. This was enough money to pay an army of a million soldiers for 8 months.
• The *Circus Maximus* (city racetrack) was enlarged for the triumphal games. It was big enough to enclose 11 football fields.

Arsinoë

## TREACHEROUS SISTER

Cleopatra's sister Arsinoë walked in the parade in chains as her punishment for joining the fight against Caesar in Egypt. The crowds thought this was a bad way to treat a queen – even a defeated one. Caesar later pardoned and freed Arsinoë.

### PRISONERS ON PARADE
*Lictors – attendants of the defeated Romans in Egypt – were paraded as prisoners with Arsinoë.*

# GLORIOUS TRIUMPH

CAESAR RETURNED TO ROME WITH FOUR VICTORIES to celebrate. Although the war had not really ended (Pompey's sons had not been defeated, they had just retreated to Spain), Caesar still planned a triumph – a traditional victory parade. To reward him for his victory in Africa, the Senate had made Caesar dictator for 10 years. The compliment flattered Caesar, but it could not distract him from the problems he now faced. The civil war had divided the Roman people.

**DIVINE CHARIOT**
*Caesar's parade chariot was pulled by four white horses – a sign of his godlike status.*

## POOR START
The parade started badly for Caesar. On the first day, the axle on his chariot broke. Superstitious Romans whispered that the gods had caused the accident because Caesar had grown too proud. Caesar believed he could stop it from happening again by chanting a spell and climbing the steps of a nearby temple on his knees.

*The crowds looked on in horror as Caesar toppled from his chariot.*

**STOLEN RICHES**
*Carriages carried treasures plundered from Gallic houses and temples.*

The Gallic triumph

Vercingetorix

## GAUL IN CHAINS
The main attraction of the Gallic triumph was the defeated leader of Gaul – Vercingetorix. He had been held prisoner since his surrender. After the triumph, Caesar had him executed.

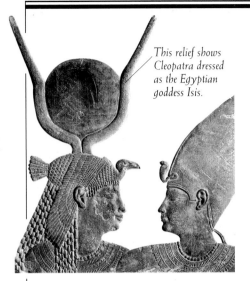

This relief shows Cleopatra dressed as the Egyptian goddess Isis.

**Rulers of Egypt**
Cleopatra was 18 and Ptolemy 13th just ten years old when their father died. When Caesar arrived three years later, they were battling for the throne. Caesar later managed to make peace between them and, as Egyptian custom demanded, brother and sister married.

A scene from a 1930s Hollywood film showing the famous romance.

**Caesar and Cleopatra**
Ptolemy feared that his attractive sister would charm Caesar into supporting her claim to the throne, and she and Caesar would rule Egypt together. He tried to keep them apart. Cleopatra delighted Caesar by smuggling herself into the palace hidden in a bedroll. The two soon became allies and lovers.

## HARBOR IN FLAMES

While Caesar's army held Ptolemy hostage in the Royal Palace, Caesar commanded his troops to set fire to the Egyptian ships moored in the Great Harbor outside. Egyptian troops loyal to the boy-king were advancing towards the palace – had they reached the harbor, they would have taken command of the ships, blocking Caesar's escape route. Later, Caesar captured the Pharos lighthouse so that he controlled all the shipping in the harbor.

# EGYPTIAN ADVENTURE

WHEN CAESAR ARRIVED IN EGYPT IN 48 BC he received a grisly gift – Pompey's head. Egypt's rulers hoped that Pompey's death would persuade Caesar to return to Rome. However, Caesar wanted more than victory over Pompey. He had come to Alexandria demanding money he claimed was owed to him by Ptolemy 12th, who was now dead. Caesar asked his son, Ptolemy 13th, and daughter, Cleopatra, to settle the debt. Outraged by his demands for money and threatened by Caesar's troops, Egyptian soldiers closed in on Alexandria, ready for conflict. Caesar barricaded himself in the Royal Palace, taking Ptolemy 13th as his hostage.

BURNING SCROLLS
Flames spread to a nearby shipment of scrolls. Almost 400,000 scrolls belonging to Alexandria's famous library were destroyed.

EGYPTIAN SHIPS
Around 60 Egyptian galleys were moored in the Great Harbor.

"BURN THE SHIPS!"
Caesar knew the Egyptian fleet would be used against him if he did not burn it.

## A NARROW ESCAPE

Two days after burning the fleet, Caesar attacked again. His troops captured the whole of Pharos Island, but a counterattack by Ptolemy's supporters made them panic. So many soldiers rushed aboard Caesar's flagship that the galley sank – Caesar escaped by swimming to a small boat nearby. Caesar freed Ptolemy – he was humiliated, he was not beaten. Months later, in March 47 BC, Caesar defeated an army led by Ptolemy and returned to Alexandria in triumph.

**PANIC ON BOARD**
*Roman troops on the galley tried to escape when they saw the chaos on the mole. They cast off the ropes mooring the ships in the harbor.*

**BATTLE ON THE MOLE**
*The mole (harbor wall) linked the city of Alexandria to Pharos Island. It was here that Caesar's troops found themselves surrounded by the Egyptian army.*

The Royal Palace

Alexandria

The Great Harbor

Pharos Island

The Pharos lighthouse

*A fire burning at the top of the Pharos helped ships find the harbor at night.*

**Pharos Tower**
The Pharos was the world's first lighthouse and one of the Seven Wonders of the Ancient World. It was so tall it could be seen 25 miles (40 km) out at sea. This lighthouse guarded the entrance to Alexandria harbor, so whoever controlled it also regulated the city's shipping. The Pharos was built around 280 BC and destroyed in an earthquake in AD 796.

**CAESAR ESCAPES**
*Weighed down by his armor, Caesar swam with great difficulty to a nearby boat in the harbor.*

**PANIC!**
*When the Roman troops on the mole realized they were surrounded and saw their ships starting to pull away, they panicked and threw themselves aboard the nearest craft.*

**SINKING SHIPS**
*The weight of the soldiers climbing aboard capsized and sank the ships.*

*Wooden stakes secured the harbor wall to the seabed.*

# Pontus and Africa

FROM EGYPT, Caesar set off for Pontus (eastern Turkey). The Romans had defeated the king of this region 20 years earlier. Now his son Pharnaces was challenging Roman rule. When Pharnaces made an attack on the Roman troops at Zela, Caesar beat him easily. Later, Caesar would glorify this easy victory by calling it the "Pontic War."

### Battle in Africa
The trouble in Pontus had distracted Caesar from the civil war in Italy. Once he had dealt with Pharnaces, he returned to Rome. In December 47 BC, Caesar traveled to Thapsus (Tunisia). There, in the "African War," he fought against armies led by Pompey's sons.

*This coin celebrates Caesar's victory in Pontus. It boasts, "I came, I saw, I conquered."*

VENI VIDI VICI

ITALY
Rome
Tarentum
MACEDONIA
PONTUS
Zela
ASIA
Ephesus
SYRIA
AFRICA
Thapsus
SICILY
Acre
EGYPT
Alexandria

**47 BC From Egypt to Africa**
After Egypt, Caesar first traveled to Pontus, then on to Rome, and eventually over to Africa.

• • • • • • ▶ *Caesar's route*

## A RIOT BREAKS OUT

The grandeur of the parade did not please everyone. Many people thought the celebrations were a waste of money, and they started a riot. Some of Caesar's troops even sang rude songs about his love life. Caesar got down from his carriage to grab the ring-leaders from the crowds.

ENRAGED!
*Caesar snatched two of the rioters and delivered them to his soldiers for execution.*

"Such a throng flocked to all these shows from every quarter...the press was often such that many were crushed to death, including two senators."

Roman historian Suetonius in *The Lives of the Caesars*, written c. AD 110

TROUBLEMAKERS
*Chanting rioters demanded that Caesar bring back the Roman Republic.*

*Sacrificial oxen with gold-coated horns were led along in the parade.*

The Pontic triumph

# Triumph entertainments

AS PART OF THE celebrations, Caesar staged spectacular games. In the forum he built a wooden amphitheater – a round arena with tiers of seats. There the crowds watched an unusual new show – gladiators fighting first with each other, and then against wild beasts.

**Circus Maximus**
At Rome's chariot-racing track, the *Circus Maximus*, there were special races in which noble Romans drove. Later, gladiators – who normally fought in pairs – formed armies to do battle.

*Central obstructions were removed for the "war" games.*

*Caesar's first* naumachia *(mock naval battle) probably looked very similar to this painting from a later time.*

**Naval battles**
Caesar invented a new kind of spectacle to amuse the people. The *naumachia* was a kind of mock naval battle. An open space in the city was dug out and flooded, and galleys were launched on the lake. On their decks, slaves and criminals fought to the death.

## YOUNG CAPTIVE

In the African parade, the son of King Juba of Numidia (now Algeria) was paraded as a prisoner. In Africa, Caesar had defeated those Romans who had supported Pompey. However, this victory over fellow Romans made some Romans angry, so Caesar claimed his victory was over Pompey's African ally, Juba, instead.

### FREEDOM GRANTED
*The young prince was released unharmed after the parade.*

# Feasting

WHEN THE PARADES WERE OVER, Caesar threw a vast banquet. The entire population of Rome was invited and 22,000 dining couches were laid out for the occasion.

**Food and wine**
Rich fish dishes and plenty of wine made a welcome change from the simple food most Romans ate.

**Relaxed diners**
Romans removed their shoes, washed their hands, and reclined on long couches to eat.

**Song and dance**
Slaves and street musicians entertained the party with pipes, cymbals, flutes, and tubas.

### CANDLELIT PROCESSION
*Elephants carrying flaming torches lit the way in the evening on the last day of the parade.*

### MUSICAL MARCH
*Musicians played as they marched in the procession.*

The African triumph

### LOOT FROM AFRICA
*Armor and weaponry from captured enemies was displayed.*

*Caesar wore garlands of flowers.*

# Caesar's forum

As a permanent reminder of his victories, Caesar set aside money for an annual triumph in his honor. He also ordered a new forum to be built and named after him. The most important building in his forum was a temple dedicated to Venus. Next to her statue Caesar erected one of Cleopatra.

## GRAND OPENING

Caesar opened his new forum as part of the victory celebrations. After the grand dinner on the last day of the triumph, Caesar walked into the forum wearing slippers and festooned with flowers. At the end of the last day, Caesar walked home, with almost all the people of Rome following behind him.

# Hail Caesar!

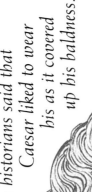

Laurel leaf crowns were worn by generals to celebrate victories. Roman historians said that Caesar liked to wear his as it covered up his baldness.

A S DICTATOR OF ROME, CAESAR SEEMED TO have everything – no one had ever held greater power. He alone ruled most of the known world, and the Roman people showered him with honors. Only the gods were greater than Caesar. But, the more powerful Caesar became, the more he was envied and hated. He was feared, too, and no man dared question his word. For the moment Caesar's awesome power protected him – but for how long?

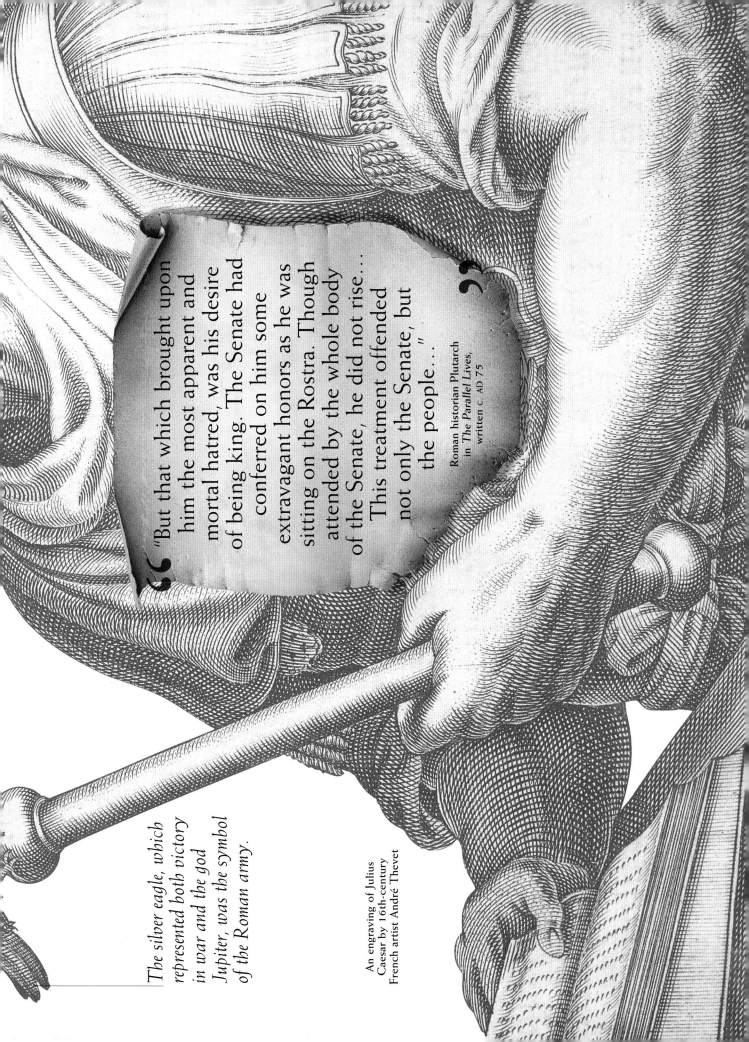

"But that which brought upon him the most apparent and mortal hatred, was his desire of being king. The Senate had conferred on him some extravagant honors as he was sitting on the Rostra. Though attended by the whole body of the Senate, he did not rise.... This treatment offended not only the Senate, but the people...."

Roman historian Plutarch
in *The Parallel Lives*,
written c. AD 75

*The silver eagle, which represented both victory in war and the god Jupiter, was the symbol of the Roman army.*

An engraving of Julius
Caesar by 16th-century
French artist André Thevet

# DICTATOR OR KING?

> "Different men at different times kept proposing various extravagant honors… to make him envied and hated as quickly as possible, that he might sooner perish."
>
> Roman historian Dio Cassius writes about the plot to ruin Caesar in *Roman History*, written c. AD 110

AS 45 BC DREW TO A CLOSE, CAESAR rushed to make long-overdue changes in Rome and the Empire beyond. He sent veteran soldiers to live in Rome's new North African colonies; he planned canals and libraries; he revised the calendar. Few doubted the importance of Caesar's reforms, but by making these changes without the Senate's approval, he made many enemies. Behind his back, and then openly, opposition to Caesar's power grew. The people whispered that he would only be satisfied when he was crowned king. Sensing danger, Caesar decided to stage a public ritual that he hoped would end these rumors for good.

**Dictator's money**
Romans used coins as a way of spreading political messages. Besides his name, some of Caesar's coins made in 44 BC were stamped with the words DICT PERPETUO – meaning perpetual dictator.

A carved terra-cotta head of a soldier from Parthia

**War against Parthia**
Three centuries earlier, Caesar's hero Alexander the Great had ruled Parthia (now modern Iraq and Iran). In 53 BC Caesar's ally Crassus had died trying to conquer the kingdom. Now, Caesar hoped to prove he was as great as Alexander by defeating the Parthians. He planned to start his campaign on March 18th, 44 BC.

CROWNING GLORY
*The diadem that Antony offered Caesar was probably a white cloth band edged with pearls. It meant much more than the gold crown he was already wearing.*

The ceremony took place on the Rostra.

ALMOST A KING
*The Senate had already honored Caesar by giving him a golden throne and by allowing him to wear the crown of ancient Roman kings.*

## REJECTING KINGSHIP

Caesar was declared dictator for life in mid-February 44 BC. To avoid the accusation that he was behaving like the king of Rome, he arranged a ceremony where Antony would be seen to offer him a diadem (a king's headband). Antony then said out loud, "The people offer this to you through me." Then Caesar rejected it, replying, "Jupiter alone is king of the Romans."

## IMAGE OF A KING

To flatter Caesar, the Senate set up busts of him near the forum. After Caesar had made such a show of denying that he wanted to be king, diadems appeared on the statues. Caesar's enemies were making fun of him. Tribunes quickly removed the diadems, reminding everyone that Caesar did not want the title "King." When Caesar heard what had happened, he flew into a rage.

*A marble bust showing Caesar in a Roman military cloak.*

# Deadly omens

IN EARLY MARCH 44 BC several strange events occured. Superstitious Romans believed that these events were omens – signs from the gods that Caesar was doomed.

### Kingbird

A flock of birds flew into the Senate house. The kingbird that led them carried a sprig of laurel in its beak, and together the birds shredded the leaves. (Caesar often wore a laurel crown.)

### Sacrifice

Romans believed that by sacrificing (killing) an animal and then examining its organs, they could foretell the future. The beast that Caesar sacrificed had no heart – the most dreadful omen of all.

### Nightmares

Caesar's wife Calpurnia dreamed that their house fell down and that she cradled Caesar's body in her arms as he died of stab wounds. Caesar dreamed that he flew above the clouds to grip the hand of the god Jupiter.

UNITED FRONT
*Conspirators agreed that each of them would stab Caesar so that they all would share the blame.*

THE RINGLEADERS
*Brutus and Cassius avoided suspicions that they might be plotting together by pretending to be bitter rivals for the job of city praetor.*

Gaius Casca

Gaius Cassius

## CONSPIRACY TO MURDER

Caesar's enemies watched in horror as his power and vanity grew. As winter ended in 44 BC, Marcus Brutus and his brother-in-law Gaius Cassius agreed that Caesar had to be stopped. They questioned other important Romans to find out who was loyal to the dictator and who hated him. Eventually 60 people joined their conspiracy (secret plot) to murder Caesar, and bring republican rule back to Rome.

Marcus Brutus

Gaius Trebonius

Tillius Cimber

*Decimus Brutus played a leading part in the plot.*

> "Beware the Ides of March!"
>
> Spurinna the fortune-teller warns Caesar that he will be in deadly danger on the Ides (the 15th) of March 44 BC. Quoted in *The Lives of the Caesars*, written by Suetonius C. AD 110

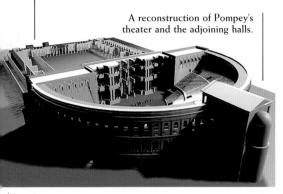

A reconstruction of Pompey's theater and the adjoining halls.

# BLOODY MURDER

CAESAR'S ENEMIES COULD WAIT NO longer. Their victim was about to leave Rome with his troops. By the Ides (the 15th) of March 44 BC their preparations were complete. The center of Rome was quiet – it was a festival day and many Romans had left town to celebrate. The plotters hoped to kill Caesar at a Senate meeting, as they believed he would feel safe and drop his guard there. They would hide their weapons in the boxes that usually contained official papers. At dawn the conspirators mingled with the other senators and awaited Caesar. They waited and became anxious. Finally, a rumor spread that Caesar was sick and would not come at all, so Decimus Brutus was sent to lure the dictator into the trap.

### Pompey's theater complex
The Senate met in the assembly hall at Pompey's theater complex, Rome's grandest building. The plotters knew that as they murdered Caesar, gladiators would be on the vast stage next door, distracting an audience of up to 40,000 Romans. Some gladiators also hid in the Senate hall in case the assassins needed help.

WARNING SIGN
*When Caesar agreed to go to the Senate, a statue of him in the hallway of his house ominously fell to the ground and smashed.*

Calpurnia

Decimus Brutus

### CAESAR HESITATES
Decimus Brutus arrived at Caesar's home to find him ill. Calpurnia, Caesar's wife, was begging him to send a message cancelling the meeting. But Brutus persuaded Caesar that it would be more polite to speak to the Senate in person.

*Caesar's litter approached the entrance to the halls of Pompey's theater.*

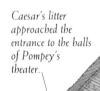

### GOING TO THE SENATE
Caesar was carried in a litter from his home to Pompey's theater, where the Senate was meeting. The people of Rome crowded around the litter, and many of them handed Caesar letters and petitions, which he collected to read later.

OFF GUARD
*Caesar did not travel with bodyguards. The Senate had sworn to protect him, and Caesar did not want to appear distrustful of their loyalty.*

### THE WARNING
A Greek teacher, Artemidorus, had learned of the plot, and gave Caesar a warning note. Seeing that Caesar was not reading the messages he had collected, Artemidorus told him, "Read this alone, and quickly, for it contains matters of great importance." Caesar started to read, but was interrupted and put it aside.

**A memento to murder**
Marcus Brutus had a new coin made to celebrate the murder. Above the inscription EID MAR (Ides of March) were two daggers and the cap of liberty that was worn by freed slaves. These were stamped on the coin to suggest that the plot had freed Rome from a wicked ruler.

*The daggers represented the murder of Caesar.*

FATAL DISTRACTION
*Cimber approached Caesar in order to demand the return of his brother, who had been banished from Rome. It was when Caesar rejected the appeal that Cimber made his first move.*

*"...being urged on by his enemies disguised as friends, he went on disregarding the omens. For it was fated that Caesar should meet his doom."*

Roman historian Appian,
in *The Civil Wars*,
written c. AD 2

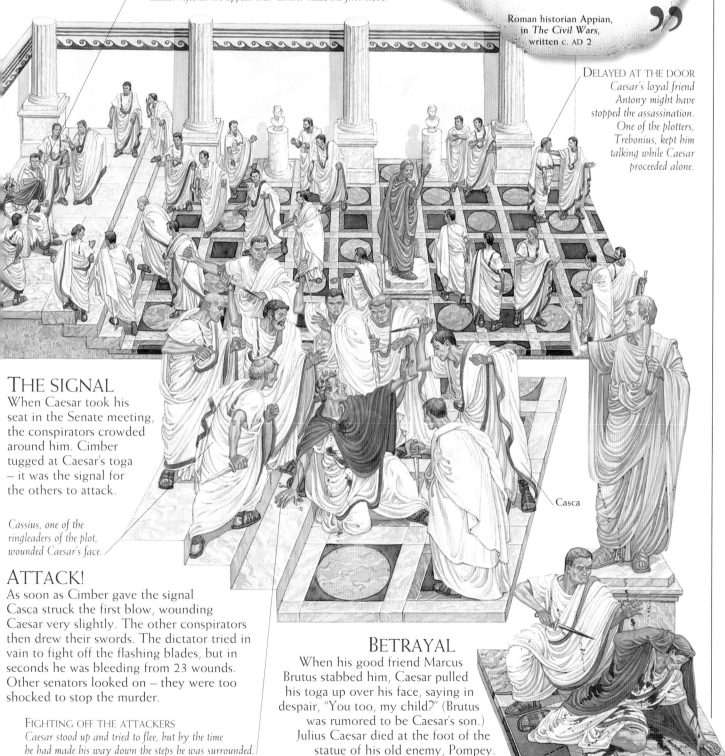

DELAYED AT THE DOOR
*Caesar's loyal friend Antony might have stopped the assassination. One of the plotters, Trebonius, kept him talking while Caesar proceeded alone.*

## THE SIGNAL
When Caesar took his seat in the Senate meeting, the conspirators crowded around him. Cimber tugged at Caesar's toga – it was the signal for the others to attack.

*Cassius, one of the ringleaders of the plot, wounded Caesar's face.*

## ATTACK!
As soon as Cimber gave the signal Casca struck the first blow, wounding Caesar very slightly. The other conspirators then drew their swords. The dictator tried in vain to fight off the flashing blades, but in seconds he was bleeding from 23 wounds. Other senators looked on – they were too shocked to stop the murder.

FIGHTING OFF THE ATTACKERS
*Caesar stood up and tried to flee, but by the time he had made his way down the steps he was surrounded.*

Casca

## BETRAYAL
When his good friend Marcus Brutus stabbed him, Caesar pulled his toga up over his face, saying in despair, "You too, my child?" (Brutus was rumored to be Caesar's son.) Julius Caesar died at the foot of the statue of his old enemy, Pompey.

**Mark Antony**
Early in 44 BC Mark Antony became Caesar's co-consul. They had been friends and allies since 54 BC. Though he was not involved in the dictator's murder, Antony realized it offered him the chance of power. Antony ruled Rome briefly with the support of the army. He was almost as ruthless as the dictator he had replaced.

> "My heart is in the coffin there with Caesar, and I must pause till it come back to me."

From Mark Antony's speech at the funeral of Caesar, in the play *Julius Caesar*, by William Shakespeare, written in 1599

**Caesar's comet**
Four months after Caesar died a bright comet appeared in the skies. It was even visible during the day. Romans believed that a comet was a sign announcing the death of a ruler. Rome's leaders at this time suggested that the comet was a sign proving Caesar was a god.

# FRIENDS AND FOES

THE DICTATOR WAS DEAD. CAESAR'S assassins walked calmly away from Pompey's theater. They were sure they had killed an evil ruler in the cause of justice. As news of the murder spread, there was panic and outrage. Brutus and his followers hid in a temple. They need not have been afraid, for when calm returned most Romans took their side. The Senate elected not to punish the plotters – but they also voted not to reverse anything Caesar had done when he was in power. The mood of forgiveness did not last long. At Caesar's funeral, the people of Rome wanted revenge.

**GRISLY WAXWORK**
*A wax model of Caesar's body was raised high above the crowd. It showed every wound Caesar had suffered.*

*Caesar's dead body was displayed as a reminder to the people of the brutality of his murder.*

## ROME MOURNS CAESAR
Caesar's body was carried in a procession to the Roman Forum, where it was laid out on the Rostra – the platform used for public speeches. The crowds that packed the forum for the funeral were sad and angry. Caesar's will had recently been read and two of the murderers had been named as his heirs. This injustice enraged the people. At the funeral, sadness soon turned to fury. Caesar had left every Roman a small sum of money, and therefore he gained everyone's sympathy in death.

**GRIEVING SOLDIERS**
*Caesar's troops beat their shields as a sign of respect for their dead leader.*

**BLOODY ROBE**
*Antony waved Caesar's bloody purple robe on a spear, like a flag.*

## FURIOUS CROWDS

As consul, Caesar's loyal friend Antony was chosen to give a speech at the funeral. He heaped praise on Caesar, then stirred the crowd with a show of sorrow and fury at his friend's murder. Finally, he raised Caesar's bloody robe. This emotional display and Antony's powerful speech caused a riot and – as he planned – helped his claim to be Caesar's successor.

"As Caesar loved me, I weep for him; as he was fortunate, I rejoice at it; as he was valiant, I honor him: but, as he was ambitious, I slew him."

Brutus explained why he murdered Caesar, in Shakespeare's play *Julius Caesar*, written in 1599

**MURDEROUS MISTAKE**
*In the chaos after the funeral, the crowd tore Caesar's friend Helvius Cinna to pieces. They had mistaken him for Cornelius Cinna, one of the men who had plotted Caesar's murder.*

## BURNING HOUSES

The angry crowd set fire to the meeting hall where Caesar had been killed, and went in search of the assassins. Brutus and the others had fled from Rome, so the crowd tried to burn down their houses. They then went back to the forum and cremated (burned) Caesar's body on a huge fire.

**SPARE THE HOUSE!**
*Neighbors and servants of the plotters begged the mob not to burn down their houses.*

**ASSASSIN'S DEATH**
*One of his friends was said to have helped Brutus thrust the sword into his own chest.*

## ASSASSIN'S END

According to legend, most of Caesar's murderers soon died violent deaths. Brutus and Cassius fought against Antony for a return of the Roman Republic. After a defeat at the Battle of Philippi in 42 BC, they both killed themselves. Trebonious, who had distracted Antony before the murder of Caesar, was himself murdered in 43 BC. After his death soldiers played football with his head.

A painting by Baron Pierre-Narcisse Guerin (1793) illustrating the death of Brutus.

# FROM REPUBLIC TO EMPIRE

WHILE ROMANS MOURNED THEIR DEAD leader, a new dictator prepared to take his place – consul Mark Antony. Caesar had named his adopted son Octavian (then aged 18) as Rome's next ruler. Antony soon made him an ally. In 42 BC they divided the Empire between them – Antony ruled the East, while Octavian in Rome commanded the West. This alliance ended in 31 BC, with Octavian's defeat of Antony. Octavian then became Rome's first emperor, and ruled the mighty Empire alone. Under his guidance, and that of the emperors who followed him, Rome grew more powerful still.

## AUGUSTUS

In accepting power in 44 BC, Octavian took on the name Caesar. In 27 BC the Senate awarded him the name Augustus. They also gave him the power to rule Rome alone. As Caesar Augustus, he repaired the damage that the civil war had done to Roman society.

A marble statue of Augustus carved c. 20 BC

## THE ROMAN FORUM

During his reign, Emperor Augustus added to the many fine buildings commissioned by Caesar. His successors built many more, mostly paid for with taxes and wealth that flowed in from conquered lands. By Emperor Constantine's reign in AD 306, the city of Rome glittered with magnificent marble buildings.

TEMPLE OF JULIUS CAESAR
*Augustus built this temple in 29 BC on the site of Julius Caesar's cremation. It was the first temple to honor a Roman.*

ARCH OF AUGUSTUS
*This arch commemorates the Battle of Actium in 31 BC in which Augustus fought against Mark Antony.*

TEMPLE OF VESTA
*First built in 715 BC, this was Rome's most important temple. The temple frequently burned down, and was last rebuilt in AD 205.*

BASILICA AEMILIA
*In Roman times basilicas were used as law courts and for public meetings. Basilica Aemilia was built in 179 BC. It was burned down in 14 BC and rebuilt by Augustus.*

SENATE HOUSE
*The Curia or Senate house was the home of Rome's parliament. This one, completed in AD 300, was Rome's fifth Senate House. Fires had destroyed the previous four.*

ARCH OF SEPTIMIUS SEVERUS
*A white marble arch erected in AD 203 to celebrate Severus' 10th anniversary as emperor. It is decorated with carved scenes of his war victories in Parthia (now Iraq and Iran).*

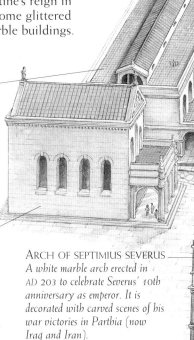

The Rostra

The Roman Forum as it looked during the reign of Emperor Constantine (AD 306–337)

A statue of Trajan once stood at the top of the column. It was replaced by one of the Christian Saint Peter in 1588.

DIVINE CROSS
Constantine was said to have seen the Christian symbol of the cross in his vision.

A painting called *The Dream of Constantine* by Agnolo Gaddi (c. 1350–96)

TINY FIGURES
Hundreds of tiny figures feature on this frieze measuring 800 ft (240 m) long.

## TRAJAN'S COLUMN

To the Romans he governed, Emperor Trajan (AD 98–117) was a wise, honest ruler who improved their city and defeated their enemies. Trajan left a magnificent reminder of his military achievements. Spiraling around his memorial column in the center of Rome is a frieze. It tells the story of his conquest of Dacia (now Romania).

## CONSTANTINE'S VISION

Romans were pagans until Constantine the Great (AD 306–337) became emperor in AD 306. Shortly before defeating one of his rivals in battle, Constantine saw a vision of a cross. He then became a Christian, encouraging others to follow the religion and allowing it to be practiced openly.

TEMPLE OF CASTOR AND POLLUX
A temple built in 482 BC by Aulus Postumus, in honor of the twin gods Castor and Pollox. It was used for special state ceremonies as well as for religious worship.

BASILICA JULIA
Rome's largest basilica was originally commissioned by Julius Caesar in 54 BC.

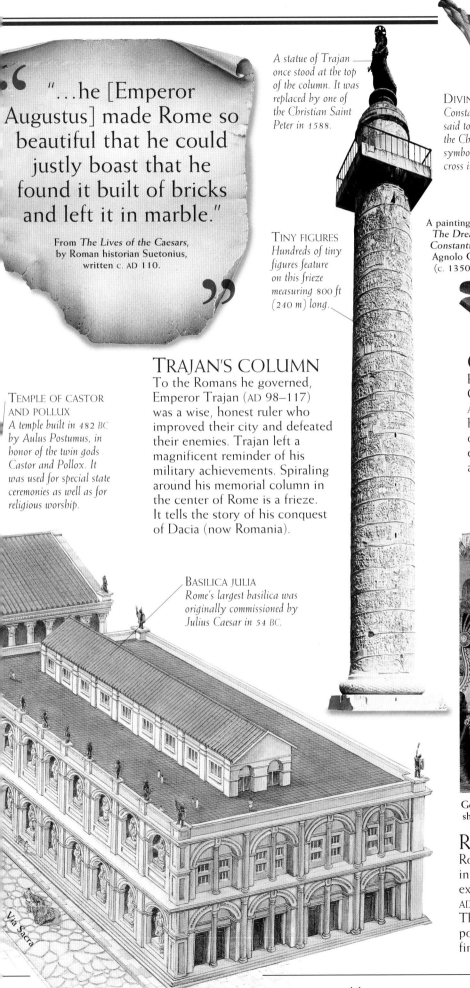

Via Sacra

German tribes attacked the city of Rome in AD 455, as shown in this painting by Heinrich Leutemann (1865).

## RAID ENDS ROMAN RULE

Rome flourished as long as wealth flowed in from conquered lands. However, when expansion of the Empire slowed down in AD 100, Rome's power began to weaken. The Empire suffered many attacks from powerful German tribes. The German tribes finally destroyed Roman rule in AD 476.

# HERO THROUGH HISTORY

THROUGHOUT HIS LIFE, AND EVEN AFTER his death, Julius Caesar inspired great interest. Some Romans continued to think of him as a tyrant and praised his murderers. Others remembered him as a brilliant leader – a man whose troops would willingly march to their death under his command. Which was the real Caesar? Was he a villain or a hero? In the 21 centuries that have passed since his birth, there have been many different views of Caesar. Historians have magnified his glory and his evil. Playwrights have turned his life into theatrical drama. Moviemakers have produced popular versions of the dictator's life. His biggest admirers, though, were tyrannical rulers, who longed to copy Caesar's successes.

## Historians

SOME OF OUR KNOWLEDGE of Caesar's life comes from his own writings. Caesar wrote a series of books glorifying his part in the Gallic and Civil Wars. For the remaining details we rely on Roman and Greek historians.

**Plutarch**
Greek author and biographer Plutarch (c. AD 46–120) wrote about Caesar in a book called *The Parallel Lives*. It compared Greek and Roman heroes.

**Appian**
Greek historian Appian lived in Alexandria in the 2nd century AD. He described Caesar's career in his book on the Civil War.

**Dio Cassius**
*Roman History* by Roman governor Dio Cassius (c. AD 150–235) is a major source of information about Caesar's life.

**Suetonius**
*The Lives of the Caesars* by Roman writer Suetonius (AD 69–122) is a lively portrait of Caesar and 11 other emperors.

*This panel shows Caesar kneeling in heaven.*

### DANTE'S HERO
In his epic poem *Divine Comedy*, Italian poet Dante Alighieri (1265–1321) describes a vision of hell. In this fantasy, Brutus and Cassius writhe in agony, hanging from the jaws of a demon. Next to them is Judas Iscariot, who betrayed Jesus Christ. Dante is suggesting that these three traitors were equally evil, and that Julius Caesar could be compared to Jesus Christ.

TRAITORS' PUNISHMENT
*Brutus and Cassius are tormented by the demons of Dante's hell.*

*Scenes from Divine Comedy*, a painting by Carl Vogel von Vogelstein (1788–1868)

Poster designed by Richard Bird for John Schlesinger's 1977 production of *Julius Caesar* at the Olivier Theatre, England

## SHAKESPEARE'S CAESAR

English playwright William Shakespeare (1564–1616) wrote a play about Caesar in 1599. Shakespeare's Caesar appears as a noble but boastful and weak man. Shakespeare based his play on Plutarch's account of Caesar's life in his book *The Parallel Lives*. The play concentrates on his murder and the events that followed.

*A gold laurel wreath was a reminder of Caesar's crown.*

*At his coronation Napoleon carried a staff featuring a Roman eagle symbol.*

A portrait of Napoleon Bonaparte by Baron François Pascal Simon Gerard (1770–1821)

"Napoleon wanted to turn Paris into Rome under the Caesars, only with louder music and more marble."

Tom Wolfe writes about how Napoleon wanted Paris to be as grand as Caesar's Rome, in *From Bauhaus to our House*, written in 1981

## NAPOLEON'S ROLE MODEL

Brutus was a hero for supporters of the French Revolution (1789–99) because he ended Caesar's dictatorship. However, the revolution brought to power a leader who admired and acted like Caesar – Napoleon Bonaparte (1769–1821). He urged his followers to read Caesar's works. Like the ambitious Roman ruler, Napoleon became a dictator, crowning himself emperor of France in 1804.

BIG-SCREEN DICTATOR
*In the animated movie Astérix and Obélix take on Caesar, cartoon artists emphasized Caesar's distinctive hooked nose and stern features.*

## FACT file

• Caesar's exploits have been the subject of more than 30 movies.

• Besides Shakespeare, four other Elizabethan playwrights wrote dramas about Julius Caesar. John Fletcher's *The False One* dramatized the story of Caesar and Cleopatra.

• The title for an emperor in Germany – *Kaiser* – and for an emperor in Russia – *Tsar* – come from the Latin name Caesar.

LOVE STORY
*Vivien Leigh played the part of Cleopatra and Claude Rains was Caesar in the 1946 movie version of Caesar's famous love affair.*

VIVIEN LEIGH in CAESAR AND CLEOPATRA with STEWART GRANGER
BERNARD SHAW'S
CLAUDE RAINS
PRODUCED AND DIRECTED BY GABRIEL PASCAL IN TECHNICOLOR

## COMIC-STRIP CAESAR

Julius Caesar appeared in the very first episode of the popular French comicstrip *Astérix the Gaul*. The comic first appeared in 1959. Though Astérix and his friends generally make fools of the Roman army, artist Albert Uderzo and writer René Goscinny portray Caesar as a dignified and fair man.

## CAESAR MAKES THE MOVIES

The drama of Caesar's life and death make them a favorite subject for movie and television adventures. The first *Julius Caesar*, a black-and-white silent film, appeared in 1908. Irish playwright George Bernard Shaw adapted his own stage play for the 1946 movie production, *Caesar and Cleopatra*, shown above.

# THE ROMAN ARMY

**M**ORE THAN JUST A FIGHTING force, the Roman army was the center of Roman society. Soldiers plundered loot from conquered peoples and made Rome rich. Army engineers created roads, bridges, and buildings to help control the new provinces. Veteran soldiers settled in the new lands and spread Roman culture wherever they marched.

**The legate**
Individually picked by Caesar, the legate (general) commanded the legion and acted as deputy to the governor in Roman provinces.

## STRUCTURE OF THE ARMY
Rome's main conquering forces were the legions – mini-armies made up entirely of infantry (footsoldiers). Auxiliary forces (foreign troops) of lightly-armed infantry and cavalry (horseback soldiers) supported each legion.

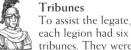

A LEGION

**The legion**
Highly trained and well-disciplined, the 5–6,000 soldiers of a Roman legion were a terrifying sight. They attacked using javelins (spears) and short swords.

**Tribunes**
To assist the legate, each legion had six tribunes. They were usually inexperienced officers who had joined the army to gain experience of military life. They would soon leave for civilian jobs.

A COHORT

A CENTURY

**The century**
The smallest unit of the legion was the century. This was a group of 80 men who marched, camped, and fought together on the battlefield. They were led by a centurion.

**Cohort**
Each legion was divided into ten cohorts, with six centuries in each cohort.

**Centurion**
Chosen from the troops they commanded, a centurion received better pay and more loot than the men he led.

**Cornicen**
To signal each new command to the men, a cornicen blew a long, curved trumpet.

**Signifer**
This was the emblem-carrier who took care of his century's savings. He could read and write.

**Cavalry**
The cavalry was made up of foreign horsemen who served the Roman army in exchange for loot.

## Roman soldier

A SOLDIER MARCHED 15 miles (10 km) a day. He carried everything he needed to fight and build camp and enough food for two weeks. The total load weighed about 66 lb (30 kg).

*A spear called a pilum*

*Stakes to plant around the camp*

*Bedroll*

*Pots and pans for cooking*

*Food and supplies of grain*

*A pickax to build camp*

*The shield is protected by a leather cover.*

**Backpack**
No one knows for certain what the Roman soldier carried in his backpack. Pack animals, such as mules, may have carried heavy tools and other camping gear.

## ROMAN BUILDING AND ENGINEERING

The Roman armies built a vast network of roads that enabled them to march quickly to the far reaches of the empire. During the Republican period, the armies also constructed bridges and aqueducts. Later, this type of work was taken over by private builders.

# Engineering tools

ROMAN ENGINEERS were able to acheive great accuracy with the simplest of instruments. Buildings such as aqueducts needed fine measurements – a small error could stop water from flowing.

### Foot rule
A folding rule like this (right) was used to measure short distances. For long distances, surveyors used long measuring rods and chains.

*Short points*

*Long points*

### Plumb line
To keep walls straight, engineers used a plumb line – a weight on a string (above). It could also be used to check that surfaces were level.

### Bronze dividers
Engineers pressed the points of dividers (above) against plans to measure and copy them. The dividers shown above were buried when a volcano engulfed and buried the town of Pompeii in AD 79.

## AQUEDUCTS
Roman engineers cut channels into rocky hillsides to bring water from springs in the mountains down to the cities. Where the water had to cross a valley, they built an aqueduct (water bridge).

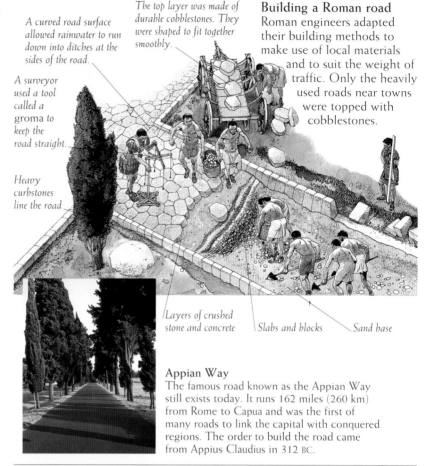

*A curved road surface allowed rainwater to run down into ditches at the sides of the road.*

*The top layer was made of durable cobblestones. They were shaped to fit together smoothly.*

*A surveyor used a tool called a groma to keep the road straight.*

*Heavy curbstones line the road*

### Building a Roman road
Roman engineers adapted their building methods to make use of local materials and to suit the weight of traffic. Only the heavily used roads near towns were topped with cobblestones.

*Layers of crushed stone and concrete*  *Slabs and blocks*  *Sand base*

### Appian Way
The famous road known as the Appian Way still exists today. It runs 162 miles (260 km) from Rome to Capua and was the first of many roads to link the capital with conquered regions. The order to build the road came from Appius Claudius in 312 BC.

### Pont du Gard
Several Roman aqueducts still stand 2,000 years after they were built. One of the finest is the Pont du Gard in southern France. Its three rows of arches rise 155 ft (47 m) above the Gard River. The lower two rows were built without mortar (cement).

*Aqueduct slopes gently downhill*

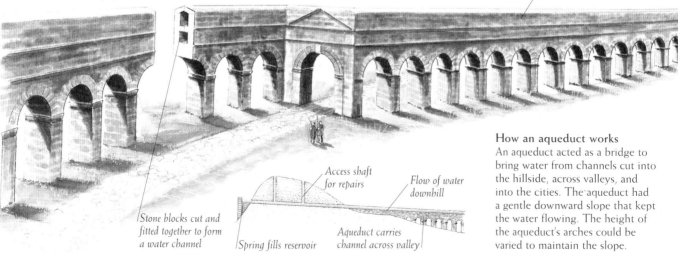

*Access shaft for repairs*

*Flow of water downhill*

*Stone blocks cut and fitted together to form a water channel*

*Spring fills reservoir*

*Aqueduct carries channel across valley*

### How an aqueduct works
An aqueduct acted as a bridge to bring water from channels cut into the hillside, across valleys, and into the cities. The aqueduct had a gentle downward slope that kept the water flowing. The height of the aqueduct's arches could be varied to maintain the slope.

# RULERS OF ROME

WHEN JULIUS CAESAR TOOK power, he treated the Republic more like an empire, and his successors ruled as emperors. For 150 years Rome grew in size and influence, and Roman emperors had great power. The best of them used this wisely, making Rome a grand city and improving life for all citizens. Growth ended with Trajan, and from AD 165, the Empire weakened. In AD 476 invaders from the north ended the Roman Empire.

## CAESAR'S LEGACY

When he was not at war, Caesar put much of his energy into building, planning, and improving Rome. He preferred grand schemes, such as the draining of unhealthy marshes near Rome, but he did not overlook details, and passed laws to keep Rome's streets swept.

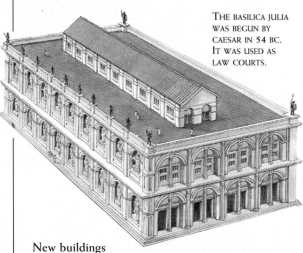

THE BASILICA JULIA WAS BEGUN BY CAESAR IN 54 BC. IT WAS USED AS LAW COURTS.

**New buildings**
The aim of Caesar's building program was to glorify his memory, but it brought other benefits too. Construction provided employment, and the public buildings made Rome a better place to live. Caesar commissioned a new forum, a people's assembly hall, a basilica, and temples.

**Land reform**
Under laws drawn up by Caesar, 80,000 of Rome's poor were given land – traditionally an old soldier's reward. The land was settled and led to the growth of towns on the southern shores of the Mediterranean, and in Spain. In another effort to end unemployment, Caesar forced landowners to use laborers, who were free men and not slaves, as a third of their workforce.

A DETAIL FROM A BRONZE COIN SHOWING THE HEAD OF JULIUS CAESAR

**Caesar's calendar**
As *Pontifex Maximus* (head priest), Caesar was responsible for Rome's calendar. Earlier miscalculations had led to the months being out of step with the seasons. Caesar took the advice of astronomer Sosigenes and added eighty days to 46 BC. The following year, and most later years, lasted 365 days each. Adding an extra day one year in four kept calendar errors down to 11 minutes a year. This "Julian" calendar was not altered until the 1700s.

**Planned library**
In 47 BC, Caesar planned a public library, and appointed scholar Marcus Varro (116–27 BC) to collect books for it. Caesar's death ended the project, but historian Asinius Pollio (76 BC–AD 4) eventually opened a public library five years later.

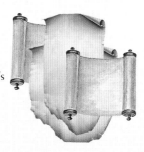

## THE EMPERORS

Rome's emperors chose who would follow them. Not all their choices were good. Many emperors are famous for their wisdom, but others were greedy or cruel. This is a list (with the dates when they ruled) of the most important of the 90 emperors of Rome.

### 27 BC–AD 14
**Augustus**
The rule of Rome's first emperor Augustus (above) finally brought peace, prosperity, and good government after the shattering civil war. Augustus was a very clever politician. He was able to keep as much control as Caesar, while pretending he had brought back republican rule.

### AD 14–37
**Tiberius**
Stepson of Augustus, Tiberius lived in the shadow of his stepfather until he became emperor at the age of 56. At first, his careful rule strengthened the Empire. However, after his son's death, Tiberius withdrew from public life and handed control to a general named Sejanus. In AD 27, he retired to the island of Capri, and never returned to Rome.

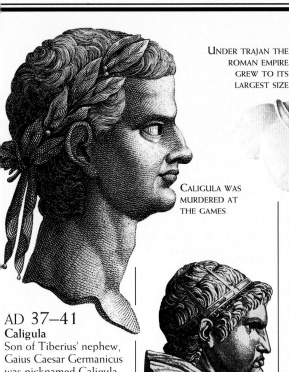

UNDER TRAJAN THE ROMAN EMPIRE GREW TO ITS LARGEST SIZE

CALIGULA WAS MURDERED AT THE GAMES

## AD 37–41
### Caligula
Son of Tiberius' nephew, Gaius Caesar Germanicus was nicknamed Caligula (little boot) by his father's soldiers. Caligula was extravagant and cruel, and probably mentally ill. He took his troops to Gaul, planning to invade Britain – then ordered them to collect seashells instead. He was eventually murdered.

## AD 41–54
### Claudius
Caligula was followed by his uncle, Claudius (above). Roman historians mocked Claudius' stammer and appearance, and ignored his important reforms. During his reign Claudius also expanded the Empire, conquering Britain in AD 43. His fourth wife, Agrippina, murdered him with poisonous mushrooms.

## AD 54–68
### Nero
Agrippina's son Nero (above) gained power aged 16. Generous and kind at first, his character altered around AD 60. He dreamed of becoming a poet, charioteer, actor, or musician, and neglected his duties as emperor. Fire destroyed Rome in AD 64, when Nero was away, but Romans blamed him anyway. He planned an extravagant palace covering a third of the city, and began building on Rome's ruins. Facing revolt in Rome, Nero fled and probably committed suicide.

## AD 69–79
### Vespasian
This popular, wise ruler from a humble family restored peace after a year of chaos. Vespasian attempted to follow the basic principles of the early Empire. His sons, Titus and Domitian, continued this tradition. Their dynasty (or family) was known as the Flavian dynasty and it continued until AD 96.

## AD 98–117
### Trajan
Spanish-born Trajan was the first non-Italian emperor. His campaigns in the east took new lands for the Empire, and he improved Rome with many new buildings.

## AD 117–138
### Hadrian
Trajan's nephew Hadrian (above) reinforced the legions that defended the Empire, but pulled them back to less distant borders that could be more easily defended. He gave large funds to help create art and architecture in the Empire.

## AD 161–180
### Marcus Aurelius
Best remembered as a deep thinker, and for supporting Rome's needy. Marcus Aurelius (above) defended the Empire from attack in the north and east.

## AD 180–192
### Commodus
With the death of Marcus Aurelius in AD 180, Rome's stability died, too. His son Commodus governed brutally and badly. By AD 192, he had become mentally ill, and his advisers had him murdered by a wrestler.

## AD 193–211
### Septimius Severus
To win the title of Emperor, Severus fought off challengers with the support of his loyal army. Troops – not the Roman people – kept him in power, so he ignored the Senate, and instead gave powerful jobs to senior soldiers. Severus was sharing power with his son, Caracalla, when he died in Britain.

## AD 211–217
### Caracalla
To ensure that he remained emperor, Caracalla (above) cruelly murdered his brother. His lasting memorial is a vast bathhouse he had built in Rome. However, his AD 212 law making every non-slave in the Empire a Roman citizen was more important.

## AD 270–275
### Aurelian
This popular ruler rebuilt the crumbling Empire. Aurelian is well known for his work to improve the distribution of free food to the poor. However, his bid to improve Rome's worthless currency failed.

## AD 284–305
### Diocletian
By splitting the Roman Empire into eastern and western halves, Diocletian admitted that the Empire had grown too big and complex for one person to rule. Diocletian made other sweeping changes, introducing fairer taxation, and a limit on prices and wages.

## AD 306–337
### Constantine the Great
When Diocletian resigned as emperor, a battle for power began among several would-be successors. Chaos and civil war ended only after Constantine (above) defeated his last rival in AD 314. As Rome's first Christian emperor, Constantine built a new capital in Constantinople (now Istanbul in Turkey), leaving Rome as a magnificent but powerless second city.

## AD 475–476
### Romulus Augustulus
Last ruler of the western Roman Empire, Romulus Augustulus (above) vanished when German chief Odoacer raided the city. The last of Rome's power disappeared in 476.

# Index

## Acknowledgments

The publisher would like to thank:
Sarah Ponder for design and visualisation;
Polly Appleton for design assistance;
Chris Bernstein for the index, and
Simon Holland for editorial assistance.

Additional photography:
Mike Dunning: 47bl; 47c; **Christi
Graham and Nick Nichols:** 35tr, 45cl;
**John Heseltine:** 45c; **Dave King:** 9br
Addtional artwork:
Janet Allis: 27br; **Sergio:** 45tr

Every effort has been made to trace
the copyright holders of written material
and we apologize for any ommissions.
We would be pleased to insert an
appropriate acknowledgment in any
subsequent edition of this publication.

Sources for quotes:
*Julius Caesar* by William Shakespeare and
*The Parallel Lives* by Plutarch. Reproduced
with permission by Project Gutenberg,
Urbana, Illinois. Website address –
http://promo.net/pg (Shakespeare's *Julius
Caesar* – Etext 1785, June 1999, Plutarch's
*The Parallel Lives* – Etext 674 edited by
A. H. Clough, October 1996).
*Roman History* by Dio Cassius, translated
by Ernest Carey (Loeb Classical Library,
1984); *Civil Wars* by Appian, translated
by Horace White (Loeb Classical Library,
1933); *The Lives of the Caesars* by Suetonius,
translated by J. C. Rolfe (Loeb Classical
Library, 1924). All published by Harvard
University Press.
*From Bauhaus to our House* by Tom Wolfe
published in the UK by Jonathan Cape.

The publisher would like to thank the
following for their kind permission to
reproduce their photographs:

a=above; c=center; b=below; l=left;
r=right; t=top

AKG London: 10cl, 26tl, 27tr, 27br;
Archiv f. Kunst & Geschichte, Berlin 41br;
46c; Kunsthistoriches Museum, Vienna
35tl; Manfred Ramstetter 45cb; Museo
Capitolino, Rome 13br. **Ancient Art &
Architecture Collection:** 8bl, 11cr, 19bl,
20tr, 34bl; G Garvey 24tl; R Sheridan
12tl, 38tl. **The Art Archive:** Archaeological
Museum Naples 9cr; Pitti Palace, Florence
42br **Bridgeman Art Library, London/
New York:** 6tl; Fitzwilliam Museum,
University of Cambridge 47bc; Giraudon
14–15; Musee de la Revolution, Francaise,
Vizille, France 39b; Museo Archeologico
Nazionale, Naples, Italy 10tl; Private

Collection 47c, 47br; Santa Croce,
Florence, Italy 41tr; Southampton City
Art Gallery 43c; Stapleton Collection
28br; Vatican Museums and Galleries 40tl.
**British Museum, London:** 37tl, 35tl, 45cl;
45cfl, 47cra. **Ermine Street Guard:** 9br.
**Mary Evans Picture Library:** 6–7, 17tr,
22–23, 32–33, 46cr, 47cla, 47crb; J C
Phillips 47tl. **Werner Forman Archive:**
8cl; British Museum, London 19tr. **Ronald
Grant Archive:** 26cl, 43bl, 43br. Image
Bank: Luis Castenada 38bl. **Mander &
Mitchenson:** Poster designed by Richard
Bird for John Schlesinger's 1977
production of *Julius Caesar* in the Olivier
Theatre © Royal National Theatre 42tl.
**Scala:** 8tl, 41ca. **Theatron Ltd:** 36tl.

Jacket:
**AKG London:** front cr. **Bridgeman Art
Library, London / New York:** Giraudon
front tl. **Ermine Street Guard:** front bc.